THOMAS
The Sand Eater

Dedication

This book is dedicated to my Grandmas Angela
Belgrave and Lynette Walker as well as
All my nieces and nephews and Kidz Corner kids
around the world
Proceeds of this book will go towards Kidz Corner
Airlines, please visit and like their
Facebook page to Learn more:
Kidz Corner Airlines
And also to YOU,
thanks for reading
Thomas The Sand Eater ☺

To order additional copies of this book, contact:
Xlibris
1-888-795-4274
www.Xlibris.com
Orders@Xlibris.com

THOMAS
The Sand Eater

Anthony Belgrave Dixon

Illustrated by Dennis Davide

Thomas loves to eat sand.

Every time we go to the park Thomas runs to the sandbox, scoops up a big chunk of sand and puts it in his mouth!

YUUUUCCCCCCKKKKKKKKK !!!

Sand is for playing, not for eating,
Thomas's mother yelled.

Thomas if you eat that sand one more time you're going in time out!

Thomas looked at his mom,
Looked at the sand,
Looked at his mom,
Looked at the sand,
Looked at his mom,
Looked at the sand and then...

Thomas scooped up a big chunk of sand and...

Thomas!!! His mother yelled, don't
you put that sand in your mouth...

Thomas looked at his mom,
Looked at the sand,
Looked at his mom,
Looked at the sand,
Looked at his mom,
Looked at the sand and...

Put all the sand in his mouth!

YUUUUCCCCCCKKKKKKKK !!!!!!
Thomas! That's it his mother yelled,
and took Thomas out of the sandbox.
Thomas was very sad, he missed
playing in the sand.

Moooooommmm Thomas yelled,
I promise, promise, promise, promise,
promise, I won't ever eat sand again!!!
Ok Thomas's mother said, sand is for
playing, not for eating!
If I see you put that sand in your mouth,
there will be no more sandbox.
Thomas was so happy to be out of time
out that he ran straight to the sandbox,
scooped up a big chunk of sand and...

Thomas looked at his mom,
Looked at the sand,
Looked at his mom,
Looked at the sand,
Looked at his mom,
Looked at the sand and...

Put it in his mouth!!

YUUUUCCCCCCKKKKKKKKK!!!!!!

Thomas! That's it his mother yelled, and took Thomas out of the sandbox. You're in time out! And once again Thomas was very sad.

**Moooooommmm Thomas yelled,
I promise, promise, promise, promise,
promise, I won't ever eat sand again!!!**

Ok Thomas's mother said, sand is for playing, not for eating!
If I see you put that sand in your mouth one more time,
there will be no more sandbox... Ever!!!

Thomas was so happy to be out of time out
that he ran straight to the sandbox,
scooped up a big chunk of sand and...

Thomas Looked at his mom,
Looked at the sand,
Looked at his mom,
Looked at the sand,
Looked at his mom,
Looked at the sand and...

Thomas made a sand castle.

The End.

Printed in the United States
By Bookmasters